BEST OF ROME
YOUR #1 ITINERARY PLANNER FOR WHAT TO SEE, DO, AND EAT

Wanderlust Pocket Guides

Planning a trip to Italy?

Check out our other Wanderlust Pocket Travel Guides on Amazon:

BEST OF FLORENCE AND TUSCANY: YOUR #1 ITINERARY PLANNER FOR WHAT TO SEE, DO, AND EAT

BEST OF VENICE: YOUR #1 ITINERARY PLANNER FOR WHAT TO SEE, DO, AND EAT

BEST OF ITALY: YOUR #1 ITINERARY PLANNER FOR WHAT TO SEE, DO, AND EAT

Also available:

BEST OF JAPAN: YOUR #1 ITINERARY PLANNER FOR WHAT TO SEE, DO, AND EAT

BEST OF TOKYO: YOUR #1 ITINERARY PLANNER FOR WHAT TO SEE, DO, AND EAT

BEST OF KYOTO: YOUR #1 ITINERARY PLANNER FOR WHAT TO SEE, DO, AND EAT

Our Free Gift to You

As purchasers of this paperback copy, we are offering you an **Amazon Matchbook download** of our colored **kindle version of this book for FREE.** Go to our book's page on Amazon and select the kindle version to download.

You **do not have to own a kindle** to read the kindle version of this book. Simply download the kindle reading app on your computer, tablet, or smartphone.

Rome is the city of echoes, the city of illusions, and the city of yearning.
Giotto di Bondone

Table of Contents

INTRODUCTION 5

HOW TO USE THIS GUIDE 6

TOP EXPERIENCES IN ROME...........................8

BEST OF ROME ITINERARIES 12

3-DAY ITINERARY 12

5-DAY ITINERARY 13

ROME...14

ORVIETO 43

OSTIA ANTICA 46

NAPLES...48

POMPEII..51

TIVOLI 53

PLANNING YOUR TRIP 55

BEST TIME TO VISIT ROME 58

EXCHANGE RATES..59

VISA INFORMATION.......................................59

ESSENTIAL ITALIAN CULTURE TO KNOW ..60

USEFUL ITALIAN TERMS AND PHRASES......61

CONCLUSION 64

CREDITS 65

COPYRIGHT AND DISCLAIMER.......................66

INTRODUCTION

Rivaled by few places on earth for its long history, Rome, the "Eternal City" was once the center of the known world. At its height, this city situated on the River Tiber, between the Apennine Mountains and the Tyrrhenian Sea, ruled over the entire stretch of land from Britain to Mesopotamia. Later, as it still is today, Rome became the capital city of Italy, as well as the host to the Vatican City, where the Pope of the Catholic faith resides.

Rome's rich cultural and historical heritage is readily apparent in its beautiful but crowded urban landscape. There are areas filled with grand palaces, towering ruins, and awe-inspiring basilicas, as well as tiny Medieval streets crammed full with shops and old houses, providing home to the city's 2.6 million inhabitants. As well as the well-known sights, an old church, or a charming fountain can be glimpsed as you turn the corner here. They are all part of Rome's haphazard charm. There is simply nowhere else like it.

How to Use This Guide

This pocket guide is centered on **Rome**, where you could spend years and still be surprised by something new and equally beautiful. When you arrive, first spend a few days with the famous ruins like the Colosseum and the Pantheon, St. Peter's Basilica in the Vatican City, the Spanish Steps, and the Trevi Fountain. You might feel like Audrey Hepburn or Gregory Peck in Roman Holidays.

After that, we recommend spending some time getting to know Rome away from the tourist areas. **Trastevere District** is lovely and not crowded. Take walks through the narrow cobblestone streets, sit in a piazza café with the locals and sip an espresso, and sample some local fare at a restaurant where they do not have an English menu. You saw the Rome of days past, here is the Rome of today.

If time allows, go for a drive or take the train to a nearby city. There is so much to see! History buffs can visit the famous Pompeii ruins, and marvel at the astonishingly well-preserved Roman city covered by volcanic ash, or perhaps go to Tivoli, where you will see two villas, one from the Roman era, one from the Renaissance. Alternatively, you can visit the hillside town of Orvieto, or go south to Naples, and feel the sea breeze on your face.

All of this and more are covered in this travel guide. You can choose to follow our 3-day or 5-day itineraries, or build your own from our detailed information on everything to see, eat, stay, and experience in and around Rome. No matter what, enjoy your time!

Best of Rome

Top Experiences in Rome

1. Step Back into History in Rome

Stand center stage at the Colosseum, and imagine looking up into the stands as a gladiator, your life about to be decided in a matter of minutes, or stroll in the Roman Forum, with your clients following you as you head into a Senate meeting. Rome is the real deal where history once took place.

Colosseum, Rome

2. Walk up to Gianicolo Hill

Listen for the cannon at midday that has fired every single day since the battle for Rome was won here. After, admire for a view of the entirety of Rome, with its old Roman part, the Vatican, and the modern city.

3. Visit Vatican City

Whether you are Catholic or not, be sure to visit Vatican City, the smallest state in the world. On certain days, you'll even catch a glimpse of the Pope on his terrace, blessing the devout gathered to see him.

Vatican City

4. Look Up at the Ceiling in the Sistine Chapel

While in the Vatican, look up at the ceiling and revel in Michaelangelo's masterpiece. There are also works by many other masters of the Renaissance in the Sistine Chapel. You won't know where to look!

Michelangelo's masterpiece on the ceiling of the Sistine Chapel

5. Meander through the Trastevere District

Allow yourself some time away from the tourist attractions, and walk on the cobblestone streets in the Trastevere District. Here you'll find the most authentic Italian fares that locals eat, and be frequently surprised by a glimpse of beauty that cannot be found near the crowded tourist sights.

6. Take a Day Trip to Tivoli

Visit Villa Adriana, the rural retreat for the Roman Emperor Hadrian, and marvel at the power and wealth of the empire at the height of Pax Romana. Afterward, visit the nearby Villa d'Este, and admire the brilliance of the Renaissance arts and architecture. Both villas have beautiful grounds for a picnic.

7. Visit the Ancient City of Pompeii

There is nothing else like Pompeii. Volcanic ashes preserved the daily life of the ancient Romans impeccably here, when Mt. Vesuvius erupted in the first century. You'll come face to face with history.

8. La Dolce Vita!

Il dolce far niente – "the sweetness of doing nothing" is an art form the Italians have long learned to master. So when in Italy, do as the Italians do – celebrate life's pleasures, relax and let the sweetness of life sink in. Eat well, drink well, admire the beauty all around you, and enjoy!

Best of Rome Itineraries

3-Day Itinerary

Day 1

Spend your first day in Rome in its oldest part – the district of Ancient Rome. We recommend buying a combo ticket to the Roman Forum and the Colosseum (the line is shorter at the Forum). Afterward, just walk around and take in the history. Each stone, each column here has history to tell.

Day 2

For your second day, visit the other well-known sights in Rome, including the Pantheon, Trevi Fountain, Piazza di Spagna and Spanish Steps, and Piazza Venezia.

Day 3

Dedicate your third day to the Vatican, the smallest city-state in the world. Book your ticket online to St. Peter's Basilica and avoid the lines. Marvel at the masterpieces that fill the Sistine Chapel.

5-Day Itinerary

Day 1 – 3
See above.

Day 4
Visit the Borghese Gallery and the Borghese Villa in the morning, for a taste of the powerful Borghese family that practically ruled Rome. Eat lunch in the offbeat Trastevere district for authentic local fare in a romantic outdoor restaurant. Take a walk there and get lost through the district's cobblestone streets. If you have some time, shop on the famous via del Corso.

Day 5
Take a day trip outside Rome. Consider Tivoli, where you'll find the ancient Villa Adriana, and the Renaissance era Villa d'Este. Or, consider visiting Ostia Antica for Roman ruins, the Medieval hill town of Orvieto, Pompeii, or the seaside Naples.

ROME

Rome, that ancient capital of the western civilization, the Eternal City, and today the largest city in Italy – no trip to the country is complete without a few days wandering the millennia-old Roman streets, and take in the haphazardly put together charm of 2,800 years of human existence, concentrated in this now sprawling metropolitan.

Rome's historical heritage is incomparable – the entire historic center of the city is a UNESCO World Heritage Site filled with wonderful palaces, churches, ruins, monuments, statues and fountains, all of staggering degrees of age. Outside the old districts, modern Rome offers worldly comforts such as nightlife and shopping. Together, Rome of past and present draw millions of visitors each year, making it one of the world's most visited cities.

Sights

Old Rome

Pantheon
As its name implies, this magnificent temple, dating back to the time of the first emperor of the Roman Empire – Augustus Caesar, was once dedicated to all gods of the Roman state religion. The building was reconstructed in 100's AD by Emperor Hadrian, who added its now widely-recognized dome, a true marvel of ancient architecture.

The Christian Church appropriated the building in the 7th century. It is the only building from the Graeco-Roman world that has remained intact and in continuous use to the present day. Under Christian use, it was formerly known as the Basilica of Santa

Maria and Martyrs, and serves as the burial ground for the first two kings of Italy – Vittorio Emanuele II and Umberto I, along with their spouses.

Standing directly beneath the oculus of the majestic dome, you can see traces of the former bronze ceiling, which was melted down during the reign of Pope Urban VIII to make bombards for the fortification of Castel Sant'Angelo.

Roof of the Pantheon

Piazza Campo de' Fiori

This open piazza, often bathed under the hot Roman sun, is used as a marketplace during the day, while students, lovers, and tourists stroll at night when it is lit by street lamps. You can find a statue of a hooded figure – Giordano Bruno, in the middle. The excommunicated Dominican monk, and one of the earliest cosmologists to have conceived the idea of an infinite universe, was burnt at the stake on this spot in 1600.

If you are lucky, you may catch a young vocalist belting out O Sole Mio at the top of his lungs here. It's a treat!

Piazza Navona
Piazza Navona, established in the 15th century, preserves the shape of the ancient Roman Stadium of the Emperor Domitian. Buildings have replaced the stands where Roman spectators once sat watching chariot races. Today, the square is off-limit to traffic, hence a popular spot to take it slow – sip coffee, shop, and people watch. There are several monuments on the square. Look for the two masterpieces by Baroque artists Bernini and Borromini.

Fountain of the Four Rivers (Fontana dei Quattro Fiumi)
Located at the center of the Piazza Navona, this beautiful fountain designed by Bernini represents the four great rivers in the known world at the time – the Ganges, the Nile, the Danube, and the Rio de la Plata. Look for the very visible Egyptian obelisk that is part of the fountain design.

Church of San Luigi dei Francesi
Close to the Pantheon is this magnificent church decorated in the Baroque style. The master Andrea Pozzo designed the trompe l'oeil dome. Look up at the beautiful ceiling frescoes.
Address: Piazza San Luigi de' Francesi, 00186 Rome, Italy

Colosseo District

Colosseum
This most famous of Roman landmarks, known once as the Flavian Amphitheater, was originally the site of animal fights and

gladiatorial combats capable of supporting some 50,000 spectators. Its name today comes from a famous statue, the Colossus of Nero, which once stood near the stadium. The massive building measures an astonishing 48 meters high, 188 meters in length, and 156 meters in width. The wooden floor where gladiators' blood once spilt is 86 meters by 54 meters, and would have been covered in sand during Roman days.

Inside the Colosseum

The line is predictably long here, but you could opt for a tour to bypass the crowd. The knowledgeable archaeologists leading the tours have a wealth of knowledge on anything you might want to know about the amphitheater. Or, you could buy a one day or a three day pass from across the street at the Roman Forum, which allows you to skip the lines as well.

Palantine Hill
This hill was once where the rich and famous of the Romans built their villas. Today you can still see the ruins of several prominent Roman families.

Roman Forum
This was once the center of Roman life – Senators gathered in the square to make important decisions for the biggest empire in the world, priests gathered here to make sacrifices, and judges to preside over cases of every kind. Located between the Capitoline and Palatine hills, the Forum is still paved by some original stones left from the Roman period. While it is less crowded than the more imposing Colosseum these days, it was in the Forum that most businesses of the empire would have been conducted on a day-to-day basis, all those thousands of years ago.

Roman Forum

Piazza Venezia

Just down via dei Fori Imperiali to the Colosseum is this enormous piazza, home to the equally imposing "Vittoriano", the monument to Victor Emmanuel. You might find it impressive, but know that most locals will hate it.

Il Vittoriano (Vittoriano Museum Complex)

Housed in the mountain of white marble overlooking Piazzo Venezia, Il Vittoriano includes the Museo Centrale del Risorgimento, which documents Italian unification, and the Tom of the Unknown Soldier. You can also take the Roma del Cielo lift to the top of the monument for a panoramic view of Rome.

San Pietro in Vincoli

This church is close to the Colosseum, but a bit hard to find. You'll be well-rewarded for your efforts, however, as you can see the chains that held St. Peter displayed before the altar, as well as an impressive statue of Moses by Michelangelo, here. Take the steps across via dei Fori Imperiali to the Colosseum, and ascend to the top. From there, just ask someone and you should be able to find it easily.

Capitoline Museum (Museo Capitolino)
The Capitoline Museum is housed in a 17th century building based on an architectural sketch by none other than Michelangelo. You'll find a number of statues from antiquities here today, including the ancient Colossus of Constantine, the Capitoline Venus, and the Dying Gaul, which is a Roman marble sculpture that copies a bronze Greek original from the 3rd century BC. You can also see the original gilt bronze equestrian statue of the Roman Emperor Marcus Aurelius, a replica of which stands in the piazza just outside the museum.

Palazzo Valentini (Le Domus Romane di Palazzo Valentini)
Just a short walk from Piazza Venezia, you can see ancient Roman houses brought to life again using state of art technology such as lasers and sound effects. History buffs will love this place, which is more than just ruins.

Modern Rome
The more modern quarter of this ancient city boasts of plenty of world-class shopping, dining options for every price range, as well as a huge assortment of hotels. It is home to the Trevi Fountain.

Trevi Fountain
This highly recognizable Baroque fountain features a mythological sculptural composition of Neptune, the Roman god

of the seas, flanked by two vividly rendered tritons: one struggling to control a violent seahorse, while the other controls a pacified creature, together symbolizing the dual nature of the oceans. Completed in 1762, the location of the fountain actually marks the much older terminus of the Aqua Virgo aqueduct, completed in 19 BC to supply the Baths of Agrippa with running water. It is named for its location on the junction of three roads – tre vie.

The tradition for visiting Trevi Fountain is to throw a coin into the water, so that one may one day return to the city, or, for the more romantic visitor, two coins so that one may fall in love with a beautiful Roman girl (or a handsome Roman boy), while three signify the thrower will marry that Roman in Rome itself. The proper way is to throw the coin using one's right hand, over one's left shoulder. The large amount of coins thrown into the fountain is actually regularly collected to finance charities.

Unfortunately Trevi Fountain is currently under restoration. You will only be able to use a suspended plexiglass walkway to take a closer look, but the restoration process should end within the year (as of August 2015).

Trevi Fountain

Via Veneto (Vittorio Veneto)
A popular site featured in Fellini's 1960 film La Dolce Vita, Via Veneto is also the location of the U.S. Embassy in the Palazzo Margherita. There are many roadside cafes to sit and people watch in.

Quirinal Palace (Palazzo del Quirinale)
Originally built in 1583 to serve as a papal summer residence, Quirinal Palace has since served as the residence for the Pope, the King of Italy, and now, the home of the president of the Italian Republic.

Palazzo Barberini
Designed by the master Bernini himself, Palazzo Barberini now houses the National Gallery of Ancient Art, where you can find

famous paintings by Lippo Lippi, Caravaggio, and Raphael's famous La Fornarina. Entrance fee is €5, free for those under 18 and over 65. *Address: (Galleria Nazionale d'Arte Antica), via delle Quattro Fontane 13*
Hours: Tu-Su 09:00-19:30.

North Center

Villa Borghese

The villa contains a garden that is very pleasant to stroll in, Rome's Zoo, a pond where you can rent a rowing boat for a romantic ride, and the Piazza di Siena.

Also situated on the villa grounds is Galleria Borghese, one of the best museums in the world, in the 17th-century villa. In just 20 rooms, you can view treasures from Antiquities, the Renaissance, and the beginnings of the Baroque period. You'll need to reserve tickets ahead of time, but this also means that you won't have to jostle for a good view of Bernini's masterpieces.

Villa Borghese

Spanish Steps (Scalinata di Spagna)

These 135 steps, confusingly built with French funds to link the Bourbon Spanish embassy to the Holy See in 1721 to 1725, are truly monumental. The climb is absolutely essential to complete a trip to Rome. You'll find tourists and locals alike hanging on these steps.

Spanish Square (Piazza di Spagna)

The most famous square in Rome, Spanish Square was the meeting point of all foreigners visiting the city, and in the 17th century, served as the residence of the Spanish Ambassador to the Holy See. There is a lot to see, including the Fontana della Barcaccia by Pietro Bernini, father of the more famous sculptor Gian Lorenzo Bernini. The name of the statue means "old boat fountain", celebrating the fact that before high walls were built along the Tiber, Rome was often flooded by rising water so high that once a boat ended up in this very square. The piazza is also home to a column commemorating the Immaculate Conception, and Italy's very first McDonalds, opened in 1986.

Vatican City

The smallest independent state in the world and the seat of the Pope, the Vatican is in a league of its own, though it is entirely surrounded by the city of Italy. Aside from Vatican City, there are also 13 buildings in Rome and one at Castel Gandolfo that enjoy the same independent extraterritorial rights.

Vatican City, Rome

St. Peter's Basilica

If Vatican City is the center of the Catholic world, then St. Peter's Basilica is the center of Vatican City. This magnificent basilica is topped by a dome designed by Michelangelo, and is of such an astonishing proportion that pictures could never do it justice. For a frame of reference, the Statue of Liberty, which is 92 meters tall, can fit easily under the dome, which has an interior height of 120 meters, with plenty of room for a helicopter to hover over.

After you take in the interior, take an elevator up to the roof, and then hike up the 323 steps to the very top of the dome for a spectacular view of Rome. This is not an easy climb, but if you are physically fit, this is not the place to be lazy and miss out. There is also a crypt underneath the structure, where you can see the tomb of Pope John Paul II.

Note that as in most places of worship in Europe, you should dress respectfully with your shoulders and most of your legs (so no mini skirts) covered, and men must take off their hats upon entering.

View of St. Peter's Basilica from Trastevere

Seeing the Pope

The head of the Catholic Church is surprisingly accessible. You can either see a usual blessing from his apartment at noon every Sunday – except in the summer when he gives it at this summer residence at Castel Gandolfo), or attend the formal Wednesday appearance, when he arrives at 10:30 to bless crowds from a balcony or platform, or in the Aula Paolo VI auditorium next St. Peter's Square in the winter.

St. Peter's Square

Though called a square, St. Peter's Square is actually an ellipse-shaped space. It contains many fountains designed by two different architects, Carlo Maderno and Gian Lorenzo Bernini. The Obelisk situated in the center was brought back from Egypt by the terrible Emperor Caligula to mark the spin of a circus, which was eventually completed by another terrible emperor, Nero.

The Vatican Museums

As the Church has always sponsored a large quantity of art, the Vatican Museums house one of the greatest art collections in the world. Ascend the spiral staircase to find the Raphael Rooms, and the exquisitely decorated Sistine Chapel with Michelangelo's frescoes. The lines can be long here, so try to book online in advance so you can skip ahead.

Swiss Guard

Their colorful striped uniforms may make them look like they belong in the circus, but these soldiers are charged with the very serious task of protecting the Pope himself. The Pontifical Swiss Guard is the oldest and smallest standing army in the world, having been founded in 1506 by the "Warrior Pope" Julius II, who also spearheaded the construction of the new basilica, and the Sistine Chapel's new paint job by none other than Michelangelo himself.

Trastevere

Just south of the Vatican and on the west bank of the Tiber is the charming district of Trastevere, the current artistic center of Rome. You'll find narrow cobbled streets and attractive squares devoid of tourists in Trastevere, which has served as inspiration to many artists including Giorgio de Chirico.

Santa Maria Church in Trastevere

The nave of Santa Maria, one of the oldest churches in Rome, is lined with an eclectic collection of columns borrowed from ancient Roman buildings, including the famed Baths of Caracalla. The apse is decorated with gold mosaics dating back to the 13th century, one of the most stunning the city has to offer. According to legend, the church was founded in 222 AD, but the building you see today dates back to the 12th century, ordered by Pope Innocence III.

Gianicolo (Janiculum Hill)

The second highest hill in Rome after Monte Mario, Gianicolo offers one of the best panoramic views of the city, provided that the city authorities have remembered to trim the tall trees that line the hill. If you forgot, you can always move a few meters down. There is a piazza and a leading up to the hill, both dedicated to Giuseppe Garibaldi, the Italian rebel leader against the French in 1849. You'll also find a statue dedicated to him on top of the hill, one dedicated to his wife, and several others to his followers in the same revolution. On the other side of the Piazza, you'll be treated to a breathtaking view of St. Peter's Basilica.

Aventino-Testaccio

Much like Trastevere, Aventino-Testaccio is an off-the-beaten-path district that has much to offer for travelers that want to get a taste of the authentic Rome, away from the crowds. But don't be fooled, because there are some great sights here as well.

Baths of Caracalla (Terme di Caracalla)

Commissioned by the infamous Roman Emperor Caracalla, these baths first opened in 217 AD and operated until the 6th century. They were spacious enough to accommodate 1,600 bathers at a time, and remain well-preserved today. During the summer months, you'll often catch opera performances here at 21:00 in the evening. You'll experience this in the truly unique setting.

History buffs should consider purchasing the €6 "Appian Way" ticket, which also grants access to the tomb of Cecilia Metella, and the Villa dei Quintilin (See Outskirts of Rome).

Esquilino-San Giovanni

Archibasilica di San Giovanni in Laterano

Commissioned by the Christianizing emperor Constantine and consecrated in 324 AD, Archibasilica di San Giovanni in Laterano was for one thousand years the most important church in all of Christendom, and the pope's main place of worship. It was the first Christian basilica built in Rome, and still serves as Rome's official cathedral and the pope's seat in his capacity as the bishop of Rome.

The church's white façade, designed by Galilei, is a wondrous example of late-baroque classicism, and is surmounted by 15 seven-meter high statues of Chris, St. John the Baptist, John the Evangelist, and the 12 Apostles. The heavy bronze doors once opened to the Curia in the Roman Forum. The interior of the church was redecorated by Francesco Borromini in 1650, and is a breathtaking sight with a beautiful gilt ceiling. Below that, a wide central nave is lined with 4.6-meter high sculptures of the apostles, and an intricate 15th-cenutry mosaic floor.
Address: Piazza di Porta San Giovanni, 4, 00184 Rome, Italy

Basilica di Santa Maria Maggiore

The ancient Basilica di Santa Maria Maggiore, sitting on top of the Esquiline Hill, dates back to the 9th century, and boasts of a beautiful mosaic-and-gold decorated interior. There is also a small museum on the church ground. On Corpus Christi (Corpus Domini), the Thursday after the 8th Sunday after Easter, the Pope hosts an early evening service in San Giovanni, followed by a procession along via Merulana to Basilica di Santa Maria Maggiore.
Address: Piazza di Santa Maria Maggiore, 00185 Rome, Italy

Nomentano
Just behind "Termini", Rome's main train station, is the vibrant nightlife district of Nomentano. Other than being a center of after

dark, the area also has a small street market with food and clothing, and unpretentious cafes frequented by students from nearby universities.

Outskirts of Rome

Abbazia di San Paolo Fuori Le Mura (St. Paul's Outside the Walls)

Abbazia di San Paolo Fuori Le Mura is the second largest church in Rome after St. Peter's Basilica, and the third largest in the world. Constantine commissioned it to be built on top of St. Paul's burial ground after being decapitated in 67AD. The original 4th century building was largely destroyed in a 1823 fire, but has since been reconstructed in the 19th century.

However, many of the church's treasures survived the fire, such as the 5th century triumphal arch with its elaborate mosaics, and the Gothic marble tabernacle over the high altar. St. Paul's tomb can still be found in the nearby confessio.

Also check out the papal portraits beneath the nave windows. Every pope since St. Peter is represented here. According to legend, the world will fall when there is no room for the next papal portrait. There are only eight spaces left.
Address: Via Ostiense 186, 00146 Rome, Italy

Appian Way
One of the earliest, and without a doubt the most important Ancient Roman roads, the Appian Way connected Rome to Brindisi in southeast Italy, and was an important route for legionary movements. Today, what remains of the original road begins close to the Baths of Caracalla, and proceeds southeast for nearly 10 kilometers. Roman tombs line the Appian Way, from those of shopkeepers and freedmen, to the more elaborate catacombs of the rich. It makes for a very interesting daytrip!

Museum of the Walls

Constructed within a section of amazingly well-preserved Aurelian Walls, on top of the gate Porta San Sebastiano, is this museum dedicated to the original construction and recent restoration of the walls. You can also take a pleasant walk on top of the walls.

Address: Via di Porta San Sebastiano 18
Hours: 09:00-14:00, last admission 13:30, closed M.

The Catacombs of San Callisto

The burial arcades at San Callisto stretch on for almost 20 kilometers long. They serve as the burial grounds for some from the 2nd century, when the catacombs began, all the way to present day, including 16 popes. Ticket is €6 and includes a guided tour in several languages.

Address: Via Appia Antica 110-126
Hours: 09:00-12:00 and 14:00-17:00, closed W.

The Catacombs of San Domitilla

Considered the best-preserved of all Roman catacombs, the Catacombs of Domitilla are the only ones to still contain ancient bones. There is also a subterranean basilica, which was reconstructed in 1870.

Address: Via delle Sette Chiese 280
Hours: 09:00-12:00, 14:00-17:00, closed each Tu and all of January.

Villa dei Quintili

The impressive Villa dei Quintili spreads over 23 hectares, and was originally built by the wealthy brothers Maximus and Condinus Quintilii. Unfortunately, Emperor Commodus took a liking to the villa, and had the brothers put to death so he can commandeer it for himself. The villa grounds include a nympheum, a tepidarium, and a bath complex, and the attached museum has friezes and sculptures from the villa. A €6 ticket will also grant access to the Tomb of Cecilia Metella, and the Baths of Caracalla.

Address: Via Appia Nuova, 1092 (difficult to reach by public transport)
Hours: 09:00-19:00 or sunset, whichever is earlier. Closed M. The web site states that an entrance on the Appian Way is open on Saturdays and Sundays but this is not reliable.

Tomb of Cecilia Metella
The Tomb of Cecilia Metella belongs to a woman who passed away in 69BC. It is the best preserved monument of all the tombs on the Appian Way, and still towers over its surroundings. During the Middles Ages, the Tomb was used as a fortress, and battlements were added. The €6 combo ticket also grants access to Villa dei Quintili and the Baths of Caracalla.
Address: Via Appia Antica 161
Hours: 09:00, variable closing depending on time of year.

Experiences

Walking Around in the Old City
The city of Rome is an outdoor museum that can only be taken in by wandering around the old city. Parts of it are still paved with uneven cobblestones, lending a small town charm to this major metropolitan. Look up, and you'll find amazing roof gardens, sculptures, paintings, and religious icons, attached to the exterior walls of the old houses. You can also look through the archway entrances of larger palazzos to see beautiful courtyards complete with sculptures, fountains, and gardens. Just like in ancient Roman days, the area between Piazza Navona and the Tiber is filled with artisans working on a myriad of trades from their small workshops.

Explore Trastevere

Trastevere, a district in Rome that literally means "beyond the Tiber River", is home to lots of restaurants, bars, and small cobbled streets. Unlike much of this touristy city, in Trastevere you can get great Italian food at very reasonable prices. There are also lots of decorated outdoor seating areas that are very romantic. Allow yourself to wander and get lost down the narrow and winding paths here, and you may find charming spots you might not have otherwise found.

Shopping around via del Corso and via Condotti and Surrounding Streets

For high-end shopping in Rome, visit via Condotti and surrounding streets, while via del Corso offers more affordable options. Via Cola di Rienzo is also a good place to browse.

Drinking in the Open

Drinking in the open has been a Roman pastime for as long as Rome itself has been around. Romans – and students in particular – are fond of buying a cheap beer from a dive bar and just hang out in a park, or take a stroll in the streets. Enjoy people watching with your drink, and experience a pleasant Roman evening.

Eat

For a more authentic culinary experience away from the tourist traps, you'll want to wander out of the historical center, and hit up a real Italian neighborhood where locals live. Trastevere is a great option.

Pizza is of course a must-try here in Rome. The pie of choice here is thin crusted, crunchier, with far less pizza topping compared to the thicker classic Neapolitan pizza. Most restaurants only serve pizza in the evening. You can also get something called pizza al taglio, which has a thicker crust and is served in pieces usually for take away. It is cheap, filling, and fun to eat as you are walking down the street.

On a hot Roman summer, grab some gelato to cool yourself down. You'll find them across the city, and they are really mostly great.

Pizzarium
$

Very probably unlike where you are from, some of Rome's best pizza is served up at takeaway joints like Pizzarium. This tiny place not far from the main Vatican Museums entrance on viale Vaticano does not have seating, but trust us, you'd be happy eating this anywhere. Dough maestro Gabriele Bonci, who has been called the "Michelangelo of Pizza" – not an honor bestowed lightly in a city fiercely proud of its art – uses specially selected

organic flours for his slow-rise pies. You can choose a classic like margherita with tomato and mozzarella, to specialty toppings created by Bonci, like ricotta, black pepper and courgettes, or vignarola, the pizza version of the Roman spring soup. Chef Bonci's bread is just as delicious if you are looking for something for a picnic.
Address: Via della Meloria 43

Osteria Di Monteverde
$
As its name implies, Osteria Di Monteverde is located in the Monteverde Nuovo area, off the beaten tourist path and therefore offers fantastic food at amazing prices. You can have a 6-course lunch menu, or visit in the evening for their 8-course dinner menu, which includes delicate but daring fares from raw seafood, and cooked fish, to meat and offal. Just be sure to save room for the great dessert.
Address: Via Pietro Cartoni, 163

Que Te Pongo
$
For a break from the carb-dominated Roman diet, try Que Te Pongo, where two guys serve up platters of top-quality smoked or preserved seafood, like whisky-marinated Scottish salmon with burrata and valerian. If you miss your bread, go for a delicious panini, which is served in baps, five-creal rolls, or focaccia bread, with delicious fillings like marinated anchovies paired with mozzarella and cherry tomatoes. The place is super popular during lunch hours, but it is actually open from 9am to 7:30pm. There are only five seats, with fast turnover, however. In any case, with so much loveliness in this city, why would you want to eat inside?
Address: Via Ripetta 40; branch: Via della Dogana Vecchia 13, near the Pantheon

Pizzeria Remo
$$

Located in the lively Testaccio district, Pizzeria Remo serves up a great Roman flat pizza with a sweet Roman atmosphere, where the chef loves to put on a show for the loud and appreciative audience. It overlooks a small park with some slides and swings – distraction for a restless child while you wait for pizza – and offers all the classic toppings. Beer, water, or soft drinks are on hand to go with your pie, but the wine isn't recommended. There are a few tables outside, but you'll probably have to wait a bit.
Address: Piazza Santa Maria Liberatrice 44

La Pratolina
$$

Just as good here at midnight as at dinnertime with the late hours, La Pratolina, just ten minutes walk from Bernini's Piazza makes their pizza from a special flour mix, with a slow, temperature-controlled rising time, and a wood-fired oven. The pies may look a bit strange to you – they are oval shaped instead of the round, which is derived from the Ancient Roman style of focaccia bread. Traditional toppings like the Genovese with mozzarella and pesto are great. Salads, beers, and wines are all pretty good as well. If possible, try to book a day or so in advance.
Address: Via degli Scipioni 248

La Tavernaccia
$$

Excellent Roman fare is served up with cheer and warmth at this family-run, local place mostly frequented by locals. For starters, try garlic bruschetta served with hand-sliced prosciutto, then move on to one of the many pasta dishes. If visiting with family, opt for the family-style lasagna. For the main dish, the variety of grilled meat and fish are great with seasonal vegetables. At dinner hours, the pizza oven in the corner and the pizzaiolo are working nonstop. It's possible to sit outside during the summer.

Address: Via Giovanni di Castel Bolognese 63

Alle Fratte di Trastevere
$$
Amazing seafood is the thing to get here at Alle Fratte di Trastevere. Located in the artsy and decidedly not touristy district of Trastevere, this place is one of the last untouched gems of Rome.
Address: Via delle fratte di Trastevere, 49/50

Roma Sparita
$$
Another gem tucked away in a beautiful, not touristy piazzas in Trastevere full of fading ochre and terracotta buildings, Roma Sparita means it's been spared from an old Rome that has largely disappeared and been replaced by the tourist industry. In the summer, sit out in the piazza with a glass of wine, while enjoying the simple and traditional Roman fare. The menu is short but top-notch. Most people go for the delicious cacio e pepe pasta with pecorino cheese and black pepper, served on a delicate shell of Parmigiano cheese, or the cozze alla marinara, mussels with garlic, chili pepper and a hit of tomato.
Address: Piazza di Santa Cecilia 24

Vascello
$$
This restaurant high up in the Monteverde area is ideally located for a reprieve from the heat in city center in the summer. It is run by two Sardinian couples, and serves up some delicious Sardinian gems as well as some of the best pasta in Rome. Try ravioli with ricotta and lemon zest, or spaghetti with bottarga – cured fish roe. Pasta carbonara or matriciana is great here as well. In the evening, there's a good selection of thin, crispy pizza and a variety of meat and fish dishes. The desserts are amazing. The torta di ricotta sells

out fast so you might want to reserve a portion lest they run out by the time you finish your main dish!
Address: Via G Massari 8, off Via dei Sprovieri

Toscano
$$$
Serving up Tuscan fare and some of the best meat in Rome, Toscano greets its patrons with a chilled glass cabinet hung with massive slabs of meat right at the entrance. Grilled beef is great here, you can get fagioli al fiasco dressed with prize-winning olive oil, or thinly sliced fried potatoes and Roman artichokes as a side. For starters, faro soup or the long Tuscan pasta pici is good, or try the tantalizing tagliolini al tartufo bianco.
Address: Via Germanico 58/60

Ditirambo
$$$
This small restaurant boasts of dramatic beamed ceilings and stone arches. You can't go wrong here with traditional Roman specialties like cacio e pepe, or try for a house innovation like thin slices of crisp potato paired with cheese fondue and slivers of decadent black truffles. The pasta and dessert is made fresh daily.
Address: Piazza della Cancelleria 74

L'Archeologia
$$$
Housed in a former posthouse across the Appian Way from the catacombs, L'Archeologia welcomes its patrons with a warm fire and walls lined with bottles of great wine. Doing justice to its ancient surroundings, this restaurant serves summer meals in its beautiful garden with 300-year-old wisteria, and 2000-year-old Roman remains. You can find anything from a traditional Roman dish to more innovative dishes here. The antipasti include cheeses and salami, seasonable vegetables and seafood. For the main

course, try a grilled meat dish served with sauces based on prized olive oil from the Sabine hills.
Address: Via Appia Antica 139

Roscioli
$$$

Roscioli started as a family grocery in the heart of Rome's historic center, which the youngest generation of the family turned into a multifunctional deli in 2002. The cheese and meat here is of the best quality, as they were in the older days. The carbonara is great, as is the gricia – rigatoni with artisanal jowl bacon, Pecorino Romano, and Sarawak black pepper. The wine list is impressive with a number of rare and vintage wines.
Address: Via dei Giubbonari 21

Il Convivio di Troianai
$$$$

The Troiani brothers have been operating Convivio since 1990, though the restaurant used to be in a different location. It is regarded as one of the best restaurants in the city, and truly a Roman institution reserved for the happiest occasions with its elegant rooms and tableware. The menu is both classic and innovative, with many traditional Roman dishes being given a new twist. For example oxtail is here served boneless with celeriac puree, combined with seasonal ingredients. You can even order a series of half portions as a sort of tailored tasting menu. The wine list is as great as the menu. The owners are always happy to suggest a pairing.
Address: Vicolo dei Soldati 31

Stay

$

The Beehive

Hostel
Via Marghera 8

The Yellow
Hostel
via Palestro 44

Hotel Prati
Via Crescenzio, 89

Hotel Azzurra
Via del Boccaccio 25

$$

Raffaello Hotel
Via Urbana 3 / 5

Hotel Opera Roma
Via Firenze 11

Hotel Sonya
Via Del Viminale 58

Hotel Dorica
Piazza Viminale 14

Hotel Selene Roma
Via del Viminale, 8

Hotel Aventino
Via San Domenico 10

$$$

Hotel Campo De' Fiori
Via del Biscione, 6

Mario de' Fiori 37
via Mario de Fiori 37/b

Hotel San Anselmo
Piazza S Anselmo 2

Hotel Diocleziano
Via Gaeta 71

Babuino 181
Via del Babuino 181

$$$$

Artemide Hotel
Via Nazionale 22

Villa Spalletti Trivelli
Via Piacenza 4

Hotel Santa Maria
Vicolo del Piede 2

ORVIETO

Orvieto is an ancient Etruscan city, built on top of a steep hill as an impregnable stronghold. The city rises above the dramatic vertical faces of cliffs, surrounded by defensive walls built of the same volcanic stone of the cliff. Just 90 minutes away from Rome, it is a perfect day trip away from the capital.

Sights

Duomo of Orvieto
The main attraction in the town, the Duomo was constructed in the 13th and 14th centuries. It is located on the Orvieto hill, and thus imposingly visible from miles away in the Umbrian

countryside. Its black and white striped façade is designed as a mixture of Romanesque and Gothic styles, but the real allure of the cathedral is inside, where you can see the frescoes of Luca Signorelli on the theme of the Last Judgment inside the Capella di San Brizio.

Palazzi Papali
Just behind the Duomo is this collection of medieval palaces, which now house the city's best devotional art. The most important piece is the marble Mary and Child sitting underneath a bronze canopy, attended by exquisite angels. A replica of the ensemble is in the niche in the center of the Duomo's façade, while the real deal is here in the palaces.

Other Sights
There are many other architectural marvels located in this walled city, including the Piazza del Popolo, Saint Patrick's well, La Cava well which dates from the Etruscan time, Corso Cavour which hosts a shop and restaurants, the medieval quarter, Saint Giovenale, Saint Giovanni, and Saint Francesco churches, Albornoz rock, and the surrounding promenade in the downtown area.

Experience

Underground Tunnels
Hidden beneath the streets is another side to the city – an extensive network connecting secret caves, dug deep into the volcanic rock that forms the earth here. Take a subterranean tour to explore this labyrinth, which has also yielded many archaeological treasures throughout the years.

Drink

Orvieto is known for its "Classico" white wine, made to the northeast of the city.

Getting In

Orvieto is only one and a half hours away from Rome's central "Termini" station by speed train. Alternatively, you can take the cheaper regional train, which departs from Roma S. Pietro, and takes about two hours.

The old Orvieto town center is uphill from the station. You can take a funicular to upper town. The town itself is easily walkable, but you can also take a minibus.

OSTIA ANTICA

Situated where the River Tiber flows into the Mediterranean, Ostia was one of the Roman Republic's first colonies, and gradually became Rome's main port. Under early emperors between Claudius and Trajan, the town expanded rapidly. It became deserted when Rome fell in 476 AD, and buildings fell into disuse. They were subsequently covered by sand and mud from the river, which preserved them. Today, Ostia showcases life in an ancient Roman commercial town at the height of the empire, like Pompeii showcases life in a slower-paced vacation town.

Sights

To get the most out of Ostia, we recommend purchasing a local map or a route guide, so you know what the ruins are.

The Forum and Capitol
The temple's podium, along with walls of the cellar where the cult statues were kept, are still intact today. You'll be awed by the massive scale of Roman temples, even though most of the walls have fallen.

The Piazza of the Corporations
Here was the commercial center of the town. Trade guilds and merchants from across the empire had offices here, each identified by its unique mosaic floor.

Apartment Buildings and Wealthy Houses
Ostia's apartment buildings are very well-preserved. They were once the living quarters of poor dock workers, and used to rise to several precarious stories in height. Today, you can go up to the

first floor through narrow stairways and corridors, and take a look at the tiny rooms the poor Romans lived in.

For comparison, visit the remains of wealthier houses, such as the House of Cupid and Psyche, which still boasts of luxurious marble decorations.

Getting In

From Termini station, take Metro B to Piramide station. The ride takes around 30 minutes.

NAPLES

Located in the south of Italy, in the Campania region, Naples is the third most populated city in the country. The city's history can be traced back to the 7th and 6th century BC, when Greeks established a colony named Neapolis, which means "new city".

Walking through Naples, you'll find the city rather different from other major European cities like, say, Milan – many buildings are a bit rundown and covered in graffiti, and the streets somewhat dirty. But whereas many of those posher European cities start to feel all the same, Naples definitely possesses a unique blend of charm not found anywhere else.

Sights

Sansevero Chapel (Museo Cappella Sansevero)
This dazzling Baroque style chapel, named after the Sangro di Sansevero princes who commissioned it, is both one of the most beautiful structures you'll see in Italy, and a little bit spooky, as it served as the funerary chapel for the princely family, and still contain a few skeletal displays in the crypt, commissioned by the seventh Sangro di Sansevero prince, Raimondo, who modified the building's style to its current Baroque, and laid the splendid marble-inlay floor.

Bourbon Tunnel
Discover your own appetite for adventure down in the Bourbon Tunnel, which had been in turn an aqueduct, an escape route, an air raid shelter, and an impound lot during its 500 years of history. The tunnel descends 30 meters into Monte Echia, and emerges again in Chiaia's Parcheggio Morelli. You can only visit the tunnel by joining a guided tour.

Teatro di San Carlo (Royal Theater of Saint Charles)
Impressively the oldest opera house in all of Europe and one of the oldest continuously active public opera venues in the world, Teatro di San Carlo is one of the Naples' most stunning sights. The theater first began operating in 1773, and still hosts an opera season from late January to May, and a ballet season from April to early June, with a capacity of 3,285.

Lungomare
Between via Partenope and via Francesco Carrociolo along the seafront is the relaxing and quiet pedestrian strip known as Lungomare. Stretching 2.5 kilometers in length, the strip offers an exquisite view of the bay, Mt. Vesuvius, two castles of Vomero's

many villas. At dusk, Capri and the distant volcano take on a soft orange hue, adding to the romantic atmosphere of this walk.

Via San Gregorio Armeno

Known as "Christmas Alley", via San Gregorio Armeno is a narrow cobble stoned alley that hosts a number of artisanal workshops that produce the famous Neapolitan nativity scenes and figures, known as "preseni". It is located in Naples' historic distric, Centro Storico, between via dei Tribunali and via San Biagio dei Librai.

Eat

The most famous of Neapolitan cuisine is something we all know and love – pizza! While in Naples, be sure to try pizza margherita, the original with fresh tomatoes, basil, fresh mozzarella, and a little olive oil. None of that meat lover Hawaiian stuff! The pizza here is going to be better than what you've had before, even in Rome or other Italian cities. Almost every pizzeria you come upon will serve a great pie.

Other than pizza, Neapolitan cuisine features a lot of seafood owing to its position on the sea. They will usually be sautéed in garlic, extra virgin olive oil, tomatoes and some kind of local red wine based sauce. Some sauce names like "arrabbiata" (angry" or "fra diavolo (brother devil" imply that it is spicy.

Getting In

Naples is only one hour away by speed train, which departs from Termini station.

POMPEII

Also in the Bay of Naples is situated the most famous ancient ruin in the world – Pompeii, which was an ancient Roman city overrun by hot lava when nearby Mt. Vesuvius erupted in 79 AD. As everything was frozen in time, Pompeii has been an excellent source for studying the daily lives of ancient Romans – from what was in their pickle jars, to where their prostitutes worked. Nearby Herculaneum suffered much of the same fate. Walk around these ancient towns, and feel the impossibly direct connections you have with people of two thousand years ago.

Sights

The Amphitheatre
Completed in 80 BC, Pompeii's amphitheater predates the Coloseum by nearly 200 years and is th earliest surviving permanent amphitheater located in Italy. In its heyday, it measured 135 meters by 104 meters, and could hold up to 20,000 spectators for the city's holidays and shows.

The Great Palaestra (Gymnasium)
In a large plot of land across the amphitheater is the gymnasium, which was used by the city's young men for sporting events, training, and swimming in the pool in the center. Colonnades surround the grounds on three sides.

Forum
As with the Forum in Rome, here was the center of public life in Pompeii. Before the eruption, this square would have been surrounded by many governmental, religious, and business buildings.

Baths

Several baths in Pompeii were preserved by volcanic ashes. The Forum Baths are well-preserved and roofed. You need to go through a long entranceway before coming inside. The Central Baths are larger but not as preserved, while the Stabian baths are interestingly decorated and present a clearer picture of how baths worked in Roman times.

Villa dei Misteri (Villa of the Mysteries)

Located outside the ancient city walls, the Villa of the Mysteries is covered in curious and finely painted frescos, some of which feature women being initiated into the ancient Greek cult of Dionysus.

Getting In

From Rome, you can catch the speed train, which takes one hour, or the slower regional train, which takes about 3 hours, to reach Pompeii. Both depart from Termini station.

From Naples, you can take the "Circumvesuviana" Line to reach Pompeii Scavi station, which takes about 30 minutes, but there are frequent delays.

TIVOLI

Just half an hour outside the city of Rome is Tivoli, which has been the location of the summer villas of the rich and famous since the time of Ancient Rome. Today, there are two main attractions in Tivoli – Hadrian's Villa, and nearby Villa d'Este. Each showcases different styles of architectural marvel, and together, they make up a memorable day trip from Rome.

Sights

Hadrian's Villa (Villa Adriana)
Stretching over a massive area of 300 acres, Hadrian's Villa was nearly a city in its own right in its heyday, and today still displays the enormous power and wealth of the Roman Empire. Built by the emperor Hadrian between 118 and 134 AD, the villa was inspired by the expanse of the empire itself, and replicates the emperor's favorite buildings from Greece, Egypt, and other provinces in true scale. While excavations of the palace grounds began in the 16th century, its size means many parts of the villa still has not been identified. You'll see many fallen columns and building ruins scattered among the ancient, lush olive groves that grow throughout the park.

Of the many buildings on the villa grounds, the Maritime Theater is particularly impressive. This was a round, traditional Roman house that served as the emperor's private retreat, built on an island surrounded by a moat that can only be reached by means of a retractable swing bridge. Oceanic motifs can still be seen on what remains standing of the building, lending the house its modern day name.

Villa d'Este

Close to Villa Adriana is another beautiful villa from a different era. Conceived and built in the 1500's by Cardinal d'Este, the gardens in Villa d'Este borrowed inspiration from Villa Adriana, as well as more than a few of the statues that used to adorn the gardens of Villa Adriana. There are many fountains, built with natural water pressure offered by the steep hillside slope that the villa is built on, and drawn from the nearby River Aniene. During the 18th and 19th centuries, the gardens began to decay due to negligence, but at the beginning of World War I, the Italian government took over care of the villa grounds and have gradually restored the magnificent park to its original state. The villa building itself is also quite beautifully adorned by frescoes.

Villa Gregoriana
If you have a bit more time, visit Villa Gregoriana on the bank of River Aniene, with ruins of an ancient Roman temple. You can wander through the woodland, and feast your eyes on a series of waterfalls. The park was designed by Pope Gregory XVI, and offers a relaxing place for a picnic that is less crowded than Villa d'Este and Villa Adriana.

Getting In

Depart from Tiburtina station in Rome, and take the Roma-Pescara train line in the direction of Stadzione Tivoli. The train trip takes about 30 minutes, but from there, you'll need to take a shuttle bus from the train station to city center, which takes about 15 minutes.

PLANNING YOUR TRIP

Transportation

Getting in

Leonardo da Vinci International Airport

Rome is served by Leonardo da Vinci (Fiumicino) International Airport, a modern, large, and well-connected facility. From the airport, you can take one of two train lines into the city.

The Leonardo Express runs every 30 minutes into Roma Termini, the central train station, and takes about 35 minutes. Tickets can be purchased online for €14, or €15 at the departure platform at the airport.

Alternatively, take the suburban train FL1 line, and get off at Tiburtina or Ostiense trains tations. From where, you can connect to the B line metro. Otherwise, get off at the Roma Trastevere train station.

But try not to arrive late at night, as you will be limited to an irregular bus unless you want to splurge on a cab ride.

Taxis in Rome are white, and take you from the airport into downtown Rome (as affixed by the Aurelian Walls) for a fixed fare of €48. This is a good option if you have three or more people, otherwise, try to take the Leonardo Express. Beware of taxis from the nearby town of Fiumicino, as they are not bound by the fixed fare rule, and you may end up paying more.

In general, make sure the driver activates the meter when driving anywhere not covered by a fixed fare. If they try to talk you into paying more than the fixed fare by saying that your destination is "hard to get to". Threaten to call the police is an efficient way if they try to overcharge you at the destination.

Ciampino International Airport

If youa re arriving from other European cities via a low-cost airline like EasyJet, RyanAir, or WizzAir, you will land in Ciampino instead of Leonardo da Vinci. It is closer to city center, but has no direct train line.

The best way to get into the city is a combination of bus and train. First, take the Atral/Schiaffini bus from just outside the terminal to either Ciampino train station – a short five minutes – or to Anagnina stop on the line A metro – around ten minutes. The cost is €1.20 for both.

From Ciampino train station, take the train to Termini station – 20 minutes – for €1.50. There are about five trains per hour.

From Anagnina station, it's easy to get to any stop near a line A stop, for €1.50 as well.

Alternatively, you can take one of the direct bus shuttle services from Ciampino to Termini. Sit Bus Shuttle runs a 40-minute bus line that costs €6 one-way, and €10 round-trip. Terravision runs a 40-minute bus for €4 one-way, and €8 round-trip, which runs every 30 minutes.

The fixed cab fare between Ciampino and city center is €30.

By Train

If travelling by train, you'll disembark at Roma Termini, the central train station, unless between the hours of 00:30 and 04:30, when Termini is closed and you'll disembark at Roma Tiburtina station instead. Other main stations are Roma Ostiense, Roma Trastevere, and Roma Tuscolana.

Budget Pass

If you are in Rome for at least three days, the Roma Pass is a good money saving option. It costs €36 for 72 hours, or €28 for 48 hours, and entitles you to free admission to the first two museums and/or archaeological sites visited, and full access to public transit within those hours. It also reduces tickets and discounts for other museums, sites, exhibitions, music events, theater and dance performances in the program. Note that for example, the Vatican Museums are not covered in this pass. Check in advance for the places you want to visit before purchasing the pass.

Getting Out

Tuscany and Florence is just a short train ride away, as is Naples, the Amalfi Coast and Sorrento.

BEST TIME TO VISIT ROME

In older days, for two weeks in August, Rome essentially becomes a ghost town. Many if not most inhabitants shut up shop and go on their own vacations, and you'd be out of luck trying to find something to eat. These days, however, to cater to international tourists, many shops and restaurants, especially in districts where sights concentrate, will stay open through the summer months. But in residential areas where locals live, you'll often see the sign "chiuso per ferie" – closed for holidays – on many shops and restaurants.

Problems finding food aside, July and August are still when Italy is most crowded and expensive to visit, as many Italians and other Europeans are on vacation, driving prices high and queues at attractions long. The weather is also intensely hot and humid at this time of year. The other times when prices are high are holidays like Christmas, New Year, and Easter.

The best times to visit are spring to early summer, or early fall. The tourist season and the heat both subside by mid to late September. In general, in April to June, September to October, you should be able to score good deals on accommodation, especially in southern Italy. The weather is less hot and humid as well, making for a more enjoyable experience. In the spring, you'll see beautiful flowers and fresh local produce, as well as a number of festivals. In the autumn, you'll have warm, temperate weather, and grapes would have just been harvested at vineyards across the country.

November to March is low season. While prices will the cheapest, some sights and hotels in coastal and mountainous areas will be closed. This won't be a problem for major cities like Rome, however, where tourists surround attractions like St. Peter's Basilica is open year-round, even in terrible weather.

EXCHANGE RATES

Unit = Euro (€)

Rates are calculated at the time of this writing. Please check before your departure for the up-to-date exchange rate.

USD: 1 Dollar = 0.9 Euro
Canadian Dollar: 1 Dollar = 9.71 Euro
British Pounds: 1 Pound = 1.39 Euro
Australian Dollar: 1 Dollar = 0.67 Euro

VISA INFORMATION

Italy is a member of the Schengen agreement. There are no border controls between countries that have signed the treaty, so citizens from those countries can freely cross into Italy. Many non-EU countries are visa-exempt. Citizens from those countries will only need to produce a valid passport when entering the country, as the stamp counts as a declaration. For more information, visit the Italian Ministry of Foreign Affairs website: http://www.esteri.it/mae/en/ministero/servizi/stranieri/default.htm l.

US: eligible for visa-free stay, up to 90 days
Canada: eligible for visa-free stay, up to 90 days
Australia: eligible for visa-free stay, up to 90 days

ESSENTIAL ITALIAN CULTURE TO KNOW

Italians are in general very patriotic, though people from different regions are proud of their regional heritage as well. They are also more often than not open and friendly, and enjoy interacting with people of every kind. Paying compliments is generally a good way to make friends. For example, tell someone how beautiful his or her town is will work wonders, especially if you can compare their town favorably to another city.

Don't be shy about asking the locals for restaurant recommendations! Italy is filled with good food, and it would be a crime to eat at tourist traps instead of sampling authentic local cuisine. Very often, the locals can point you to their favorite spots off the beaten path, which will be cheaper and tastier than what you can find on your own in the touristy areas.

Theft is a common problem, especially in large cities like Rome. Rome is full of pickpocket, though violent crimes are rare. In public areas, crowded metros and buses, hold onto your handbags and wallets. Men should avoid putting their wallets in their back pockets. You should also watch out for gypsies.

USEFUL ITALIAN TERMS AND PHRASES

In larger cities, you'll likely find someone who speaks English, but in a small town or less touristy areas, it'll be helpful to have some Italian phrases.

Do you speak English: Parla Inglese?

Thank You: Grazie.

You are welcome: Prego.

Please: Per favore; Per Piacere.

Good Morning/Good Afternoon: Buon Giorno.

Good Evening: Buona Sera.

Good Night: Buona note.

How are you (singular): Come sta?

How are you (plural): Come state?

Excuse me: Mi scusi/Scusi.

Hello/Goodbye: Ciao.

How much does it cost: Quanto costa?

Where is ...: Dov'è ....?

Lavatory/Toilet: Gabinetto/Bagno.

To eat: Mangiare

Where is the ... Embassy: Dove si trova... l'ambasciata?

Restaurant: Ristorante.

Stamp: Francobollo.

Postcard: Cartolina.

May I take photos: Posso fare fotografie?

Where can I find a...: Dove posso trovare un.../

I have a booking/we have a booking: Ho una prenotazione/Abbiamo una prenotazione.

Would like something to eat: Vorrei qualcosa da mangiare.

I would like something to drink: Vorrei qualcosa da bere.

How can I go to...: Come posso andare a...

I am allergic to...: Sono allergico a...

Do you accept credit cards: Accettate carte di credito?

Prescription: Prescrizione/Ricetta.

May I pay at check-out: Posso pagare al check-out?

Check please: Il conto, per favore.

Is there internet connection: C'è la connessione ad internet.

How much does it cost? / How much does this cost: Quanto costa? / Quanto costa questo?

Police: Polizia/Carabinieri.

Taxi: Taxi.

Bus stop: Fermata dell'autobus.

Airport: Aeroporto.

Train station: Stazione.

Pharmacy: Farmacia.

Doctor: Medico.

Hotel: Albergo/Hotel.

Pain: Dolore.

Blisters: Vesciche.

Food store: Supermercato.

Shop: Negozio.

Hospital: Ospedale.

Emergency room: Pronto soccorso.

Museum: Museo.

Ticket desk: Biglietteria.

Guidebook: Guida turistica.

Guided tour: Visita guidata.

Opening time: Orario di aperture.

Go away: Vai via!

CONCLUSION

We hope this pocket guide helps you navigate Rome, and find the most memorable and authentic things to do, see, and eat.

Thank you for purchasing our pocket guide. After you've read this guide, we'd really appreciate your honest book review!

Sincerely,
The Wanderlust Pocket Guides Team

CREDITS

Cover design by Wanderlust Pocket Guide Design Team

Made in the USA
San Bernardino, CA
14 March 2017